G000168763

This copy of
The Vampire Joke Book
belongs to.............

Also in Beaver by Peter Eldin

Skool Graffitti
The Woolly Jumper Joke Book

THE VAMPIRE JOKE BOOK

Peter Eldin

Illustrated by Jean Baylis

Beaver Books

A Beaver Book
Published by Arrow Books Limited
62–5 Chandos Place, London WC2N 4NW

An imprint of Century Hutchinson Ltd

London Melbourne Sydney Auckland
Johannesburg and agencies throughout the world

First published 1987

Set in Baskerville
by JH Graphics Ltd, Reading

Made and printed in Great Britain
by Anchor Brendon Ltd
Tiptree, Essex

ISBN 0 09 954130 0

From ghoulies and ghosties
and long-leggety beasties,
The Vampire Joke Book
and things that go bump in the night,
Good Lord, deliver us.

(traditional Scottish prayer)

What is a vampire's favourite soup?
Scream of tomato.

What happens when you meet twin witches?
You can't tell which witch is which.

What is a vampire's favourite hobby?
In-grave-ing.

RICK: What's the difference between a vampire and a letter box?
MICK: *I don't know.*
RICK: Well, if that's the case I'm not going to let you post any of my letters.

What did the werewolf say when he saw two werewolf hunters in a Land Rover?
'Meals on wheels!'

How does a witch tell the time?
She looks at her witch watch.

What did the policeman say when he met a three-headed monster?
'Hello, hello, hello.'

Mummy, Mummy, what's for dinner?
Shut up and get back in the oven.

What does a ghost like to drink?
Bier.

A man was standing in the middle of the road spreading powder all over it.
A policeman spotted him and asked him what he was doing.
'I'm spreading anti-vampire powder around,' said the man.
'But there aren't any vampires around here,' said the policeman.
'That just proves how effective the powder is!' the man replied.

What does the Devil like to drink?
Demonade.

What is a monster's favourite kind of soup?
One with plenty of body in it.

What is fearsome and hairy and goes up and down?
A werewolf in a lift.

PETE: My dad once came face to face with a horrific vampire and he didn't turn a hair.
RICK: *I'm not surprised — your dad is bald.*

Who is a ghost's favourite musician?
James Ghoulway.

What monster makes noises in its throat?
A gargoyle.

Why do witches travel on broomsticks?
Because the flex on their vacuum cleaners is too short.

How would you describe a group of monsters parading along a street?
A demon-stration.

Why don't skeletons do much work?
Because they are bone idle.

What's a skeleton's favourite vegetable?
Marrow.

What do you get if you cross a monster with a mouse?
Great big holes in the skirting board.

What kind of tunes do ghosts like?
Haunting melodies.

Who is in charge of the ghost squad?
An inspectre.

What jewels do ghosts wear?
Tomb stones.

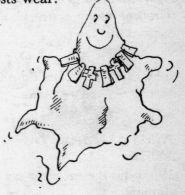

Where do American ghosts go fishing?
Lake Eerie.

What do you give King Kong when he is sick?
Plenty of room.

Why do witches get stiff joints?
They catch broomatism.

What do you give a monster with big feet?
Plenty of room.

What did the monster say when he was late for dinner?
'Has everyone been eaten already?'

What do you call a wicked old hag who lives on a beach?
A sandwitch.

What would you call two drunk ghosts?
Methylated spirits.

FRED: If a werewolf's head is pointing north, where would his tail be pointing?
TED: *To the south.*
FRED: No, to the ground.

What is a witch's favourite meal?
Toad in the hole.

Why are ghosts very simple things?
Because they can easily be seen through.

What do short-sighted ghosts wear?
Spooktacles.

Which American president ate people?
Jaws Washington.

Did you hear about the monster on a diet?
He only eats pygmies.

What do you call a ghostly French emperor?
Napoleon Boney-parte.

What is the phantom navy called?
The ghost guard.

What haunts a school?
The school spirit.

What is a ghost writer?
A spooksman.

Why is Dracula a bore?
Because he is a pain in the neck.

How can you tell there's a monster under your bed?
Your nose is pressed against the ceiling.

How can you stop monsters from hiding under your bed?
Cut the legs off the bed.

On which day of the week are you more likely to be eaten by a monster?
Chewsday.

Why did the monster decide to become a vegetarian?
He was fed up with people.

What do you call a short vampire?
A pain in the knee.

What should you do with a blue monster?
Try to cheer him up.

What should you do if you come face to face with Dracula, Frankenstein's Monster, King Kong, and a mummy?
Hope that you are at a fancy dress party.

What did one Invisible Man say to the other Invisible Man?
'It's nice not to see you again.'

What does a ghost wear when it is raining?
Ghouloshes.

What does a ghost wear when it is raining?
Boo-oots.

How did the witch travel from Land's End to John O'Groats?
She witch-hiked.

What's a skeleton?
A man with his outsides off and his insides out.

How can you tell when a ghost is ill?
It goes as white as a sheet.

FIRST GHOST TO SECOND GHOST: Do you
believe in people?

Who serves spirits on an aeroplane?
The air ghostess.

What do you get when you cross a monster with
a boy scout?
A monster who helps old ladies across the road.

What overweight monster lives in the
Opera House?
The Fat-tum of the Opera.

Would you rather King Kong ate you or that a
werewolf ate you?
I'd rather King Kong ate the werewolf.

What do ghost busters write in?
Exorcise books.

On which side does a werewolf have most hair?
On the outside.

What do you call a vampire wearing earmuffs?
Anything you like. He can't hear you.

MOTHER MONSTER: Why did you put a frog in
your sister's bed?
BOY MONSTER: *Because I couldn't find a mouse.*

What's the best way to catch a monster?
Get someone to throw one to you.

What did the barman say to the ghost?
'Sorry, but we don't serve spirits.'

Where does a ghost train stop?
At a manifestation.

Why did the Invisible Man look in the mirror?
To make sure he still wasn't there.

What time was it when the werewolf ate the Prime Minister?
Ate p.m.

Miss Aaargh won this year's monster beauty contest.
Her measurements are 36.27.35 . . .
35.28.38. . . . and 78.56.81!

Why is Dracula a good person to take out to dinner?
Because he eats necks to nothing.

What do you call a duck with fangs?
Count Quakula.

Why did the ghost keep measuring himself?
He wanted to know when he gruesome.

Which monster is good at subtraction?
The Loch Less Monster.

Which monster is very unlucky?
The Luck Less Monster.

Which monster is very untidy?
The Loch Mess Monster.

Where does Dracula have his American office?
In the Vampire State Building.

When do ghosts play jokes on each other?
April Ghoul's Day.

CHARLIE: What would you say if you saw a
    ghost?
BENNY: *I wouldn't say anything, I'd just run.*

Mummy, Mummy, what's a vampire?
Be quiet and drink your blood.

Where do Spanish ghosts go on holiday?
The Ghosta Brava.

What is a skeleton?
Bones with the person off.

What goes oob, oob?
A ghost walking backwards.

What did the mother ghost say to her talkative son?
'Spook when you're spooken to.'

What would you get if you crossed a werewolf with a parrot?
Something that will bite your leg off and then say 'Who's a pretty boy?'

What colour comes to mind when you meet a monster?
Yell-oh.

What time is it when a ten foot high monster sits on your fence?
Time to get a new fence.

What would a witch do if she swallowed a frog?
She might croak.

What sort of plates do skeletons like to eat off?
Bone china.

What is a vampire's favourite fruit?
A nectarine.

What do you get if you cross a werewolf with a flower?
I don't know, but I wouldn't recommend smelling it.

What is King Kong's favourite Christmas song?
Jungle bells, jungle bells.

What film musical was written by the friend of a giant ape?
The Kong and I.

Where are monsters found?
I don't know. It's not very often that they get lost.

Mummy, Mummy, why is Daddy so still?
Shut up, and keep digging.

Why isn't Dracula married?
Because he is a bat-chelor.

If you were walking in Transylvania and you saw Dracula what time would it be?
Time to run.

Who is a vampire likely to fall in love with?
The girl necks door.

What's a monster's favourite meal?
Baked beings on toast.

What does Frankenstein's monster call a screwdriver?
Daddy.

What happens if you cross a sheep with a werewolf?
You have to get a new sheep.

What do you call a haunted wigwam?
A creepy teepee.

What do you call a kind, handsome, vegetarian monster?
A failure.

Did you hear about the prehistoric monster who took an exam?
He passed with extinction.

I used to be a werewolf but I'm all right now-oooow.

Where does Dracula get all his jokes?
From his crypt writer.

Why do ghosts pack their cases in the summer?
They are getting ready for their horrordays.

Did you hear about the vegetarian werewolf?
He would only eat Swedes.

How can you tell a thirty stone monster from a banana?
Try picking it up. If you can't, it's probably the monster.

What was the name of a famous Scottish skeleton?
Boney Prince Charlie.

What do you call an idle skeleton?
Lazy bones.

What is big, green and miserable?
The Incredible Sulk.

What's the difference between a werewolf and a flea?
The werewolf can have fleas but the flea can't have werewolves.

How do monsters like their eggs?
Terri-fried.

Why did Dracula become an actor?
He wanted a part that he could get his teeth into.

What is Dracula's favourite breed of dog?
A bloodhound.

Where do ghosts go for their holidays?
Boo York.

What did the monster say after he had eaten a roll of film?
'I enjoyed the book better.'

What is red, sweet and bites people in the neck?
A jampire.

A ten foot high monster with long arms and
two legs of different lengths walked into a
tailor's shop.
'I'd like to see a suit that would fit me,' he
said.
'So would I!' said the tailor.

A vampire, a witch and a werewolf were trying
to shelter beneath an umbrella but not one of
them got wet. Why not?
It wasn't raining.

What is a spook's favourite ride in an amusement park?
The roller ghoster.

What is a young ghost's favourite television programme?
Boo Peter.

FIRST MONSTER: Why are you standing on one leg?
SECOND MONSTER: *Because you just trod on my foot.*

Where did the witch have her hair done?
At the ugly parlour.

What do you call a well-dressed hairy beast?
A wear-wolf.

What do you call a lost hairy beast?
A where-wolf.

What do you get if you cross a friend with a dead Egyptian?
A chummy mummy.

What do you call a hairy beast that no longer exists?
A were-wolf.

What do you call a hairy beast in a river?
A weir-wolf.

What is made of bread and meat, is wrapped up in cellophane and rings bells in Paris?
The Lunchpack of Notre Dame.

Why did the vampire fly over the mountain?
Because he couldn't fly under it.

What sort of eyes do monsters have?
Terror-ise.

In the Egyptian room of the museum Bert
and Gert stopped to look at a mummy. In
front of the case was a sign that said
'2356 BC'.
'What does that 2356 BC mean?' asked Gert.
Bert thought for a moment and then said
'Oh, that's probably the number of the car
that hit him.'

DAN: I hear you've just come back from Tibet.
PETE: *That's right. And one day I was taken out yeti hunting.*
DAN: Any luck?
PETE: *Yes . . . we didn't meet any!*

What's the difference between a vampire with toothache and a rainstorm?
One roars with pain and the other pours with rain.

Can a vampire jump higher than a house?
Of course. A house can't jump.

What does a vampire have that no other creature has?
Baby vampires.

How do you get a thirty stone monster into a matchbox?
Take all the matches out first.

FIRST MONSTER: Have you tried the new Chinese take-away?
SECOND MONSTER: *No, when I went there they'd run out of Chinamen.*

Two thirty stone monsters fell over a cliff — boom, boom.

What would you get if you crossed a pig with a thirty stone monster?
Big pork chops.

What does a vampire do when it rains?
He gets wet.

FIRST UNDERTAKER: How's business?
SECOND UNDERTAKER: *Same as usual . . . dead.*

Where does an undertaker carry on his business?
In a box office.

FIRST MONSTER: I've just eaten a human skeleton.
SECOND MONSTER: *Are you choking?*
FIRST MONSTER: No, I'm being serious.

What is the undertaker's motto?
The morgue the merrier.

What did the werewolf say after he'd eaten a clown?
'I feel funny.'

What do you call a detective skeleton?
Sherlock Bones.

The Invisible Man's son wants to follow in his father's footsteps. There's just one problem — he can't find them!

How do ghosts get through closed doors?
They use skeleton keys.

Where do ghosts go for their holidays?
To Wails.

Who won the monster's beauty contest?
No-one.

What's the difference between a witch and the letters K, M, A, S, E?
One makes spells and the other spells 'makes'.

MOTHER MONSTER TO BABY MONSTER: How many times have I told you not to speak with your mouths full?

The Invisible Man went out for a walk with his son. There's just one problem — if he was invisible how did his parents know he was a boy?

Why did the ghost go to Africa?
He wanted to become a big game haunter.

What is Dracula's favourite drink?
A Bloody Mary.

What do you call a phantom chicken?
A poultry-geist.

What do you call a failed phantom?
A paltry-geist.

What do you call a Polish phantom?
A Pole-tergeist.

What do you call a ghost who is a candidate in a General Election?
A poll-tergeist.

What do werewolves like to eat with bread and cheese?
Pickled organs.

What relationship is Dracula to Frankenstein?
They are blood brothers.

Why did the ghost go to the party?
To have a wail of a time.

What did the ghost stewardess say to her passengers?
'Fasten your sheet belts.'

What did the monster do when he lost a hand?
He went to a second hand shop.

Why was Frankenstein's monster told off at the dinner table?
Because he bolted his food.

What walks through walls going 'Er . . . boo'?
A nervous ghost.

Why do they put a fence around graveyards?
Because people are dying to get in.

Why didn't the monster eat the priest?
Because he knew that you can't keep a good man down.

What would you call a skeleton who goes out in the cold without a hat?
A numb skull.

What do you call an old and foolish vampire?
A silly old sucker.

Why did the ghost have to go to hospital?
To have his ghoulstones removed.

What did the monster do when he lost a tail?
He went to a re-tailer.

What would you call a ghost shepherdess?
Little Boo Peep.

Why did the undertaker go to Olympia?
To see The Hearse of the Year Show.

What's the difference between a small witch and
a deer on the run?
One's a stunted hag and the other's a hunted stag.

A horrific monster, with three heads, seven
eyes, two tails and long claws walked into a
pub and ordered a pint of beer.
'That will be £3.50, please,' said the barman.
After a while the barman overcame his
revulsion at the sight of the horrific monster
and said: 'Excuse me for saying so, but we
don't get many monsters here.'
'I'm not surprised,' said the monster, 'With
beer at £3.50 a pint!'

Why did the ghost jump when his mother-in-law
called?
Because he did not ex-spectre.

What did the Invisible Man call his mother and
father?
His transparents.

How do monsters count up to fourteen?
On their fingers.

What did the ghost buy his wife for Christmas?
A see-through nightdress.

YOUNG MONSTER: Mummy, I don't like Daddy.
MOTHER MONSTER: *Try putting some more salt on.*

What type of photographs does the Invisible Man take?
Transparencies.

Why did the monster get indigestion?
He'd eaten somone who disagreed with him.

SAM: My dad's a vampire hunter in Ireland.
DAN: *But there aren't any vampires in Ireland.*
SAM: Not now there aren't. My dad shot them all.

What would a witch do if she wanted to diet?
She'd go to weight witches.

What is Dracula's favourite song?
Fangs for the Memory.

Who delivers presents to werewolves at Christmas?
Santa Claws.

Why is Dracula big-headed?
Because he is a vein person.

Why are ghosts regarded as cowards?
Because they've got no guts.

What do Italian ghosts eat?
Spookhetti.

When did the vampire fall down?
When he veinted.

Why did the headless coachman take some hay
to bed with him?
To feed his night mares.

Why was the bicycle haunted?
It had spooks in its wheels.

Who has the most dangerous job in Transylvania?
Dracula's dentist.

YOUNG MONSTER: Mum, I hate my sister's guts.
MOTHER MONSTER: *Stop complaining and eat what's on your plate.*

What do racing witches ride on?
Vroomsticks.

Why was the ten-legged monster late for work?
He spent all morning putting his shoes on.

Why was the vampire upset?
He'd just received a letter from the manager of the blood bank telling him that he was nine pints overdrawn.

How did the monster feel after he'd eaten a sheep?
Ba-a-a-d.

What did the sentry call out when he was on duty in Transylvania?
'Who goes there? Fiend or foe?'

What do you call ghosts on a mountain?
High spirits.

FIRST VAMPIRE HUNTER: Yesterday a vampire bit my neck.

SECOND VAMPIRE HUNTER: *Did you put anything on it?*

FIRST VAMPIRE HUNTER: No, he seemed to like it just as it was.

What do you call a lazy stegosaurus?
A stegosnaurus.

What's the difference between a werewolf and a flea?
One howls on the prairie, the other prowls on the hairy.

What is an American ghost's favourite dessert?
Boo-berry pie.

FIRST MONSTER: How do you know the monster hunter has been eaten?

SECOND MONSTER: *I've got inside information.*

How do British ghosts travel abroad?
By British Scareways.

What is a ghost's favourite position in football?
Ghoulkeeper.

JIM: What have I got in my hand?
SLIM: *A twelve foot high monster.*
JIM: You peeped!

MALE MONSTER: You have such lovely eyes.
FEMALE MONSTER: *Yes, they were given to me as a birthday present.*

What's the difference between a sick monster and a dead bee?
One's a seedy beast and the other is a bee deceased.

MOTHER MONSTER TO TEENAGE SON: If your father could see you now he'd turn in his gravy.

What sort of monster gets up your nose?
A bogeyman.

What do you call the flying ghost of a sailor?
A sea ghoul.

What would you find in a haunted cellar?
Whines and spirits.

What is a vampire after he is ten days old?
Eleven days old.

Who teaches young ghosts?
A ghoulmaster.

What's a monster's favourite party game?
Swallow my leader.

What happened when the thirty stone monster
married a twenty stone monster?
They had a big wedding.

What did the river say when the thirty stone
monster sat in it?
'Well, I'm dammed!'

MOTHER MONSTER: Why did you drop the baby on the floor?

GIRL MONSTER: *Well, you said he was a bonny bouncing baby, so I wanted to see if he did.*

What do vampire sailors sail in?
Blood vessels.

Why was the cowardly vampire such a failure?
Because he fainted at the sight of blood.

What did the undertaker call his funeral parlour?
The Departure Lounge.

What do you call a daft vampire?
A silly clot.

Why couldn't the witch sing?
She had a frog in her throat.

I have five eyes, two heads, three ears and two fangs. What am I?
Ugly.

When would a vampire invite you to lunch?
When he fancied a bite.

How do you know when you are in bed with a monster?
He has an 'M' on his pyjamas.

What do you call a clever monster?
Frank Einstein.

Why is a graveyard never empty?
Because there's always some body in it.

What is a vampire's favourite dessert?
I scream.

Why did the werewolves call their son 'Camera'?
Because he was always snapping.

FIRST MONSTER: Does you wife cook best by gas or electricity?
SECOND MONSTER: *I don't know, I've never tried to cook her.*

When he was in court what did the vampire promise?
To tell the tooth, the whole tooth and nothing but the tooth.

What happened when the thirty stone monster died?
He was buried — but it was a huge undertaking.

What do you do if King Kong sits in front of you at the cinema?
Miss most of the film.

Where does a ten foot monster sleep?
Anywhere it likes.

How does a ghost find his way when he is lost?
He uses dead reckoning.

Which ghost was President of France?
Charles de Ghoul.

What's the difference between a vampire and a biscuit?
You can't dunk a vampire in your tea.

Where do ghosts like to go swimming?
In the Dead Sea.

What is the ghosts' national anthem?
Ghoul Britannia.

What aftershave do monsters use?
Brute.

Why are werewolves regarded as quick witted?
Because they always give snappy answers.

What would you call a stupid monster?
A dummy mummy.

What does Dracula have at eleven o'clock every morning?
A coffin break.

Why was Dracula always willing to help young vampires?
Because he liked to see new blood in the business.

Why can you trust a mummy with a secret?
Because they always keep everything under wraps.

FIRST MONSTER: How did the monster hunter go down?
SECOND MONSTER: *Great. We've ordered another one for Christmas.*

What would you get if you crossed a werewolf with your pet dog?
A nervous postman.

What do witches say when they overtake each other?
'Broom, broom, broom.'

What should you do if you find a monster sleeping in your bed?
Sleep somewhere else.

What is as big as a thirty stone monster but doesn't weigh an ounce?
The monster's shadow.

What's an English monster's favourite meal?
Kate and Sidney pie.

What is an African monster's favourite meal?
Snake and pygmy pie.

What kind of sandals does a witch wear?
Open-toed.

What is Dr Jekyll's favourite game?
Hyde and seek.

Why did the monster subscribe to *Which*?
He wanted to be a member of the Consumers' Association.

Knock, knock.
Who's there?
Ivan.
Ivan who?
Ivan to bite your neck.

Why did King Kong wear sunglasses?
He didn't want to be recognized.

What happened to Frankenstein's monster when
he was found guilty of a crime?
He was dismantled for six months.

What do monsters like to read in the newspapers?
Their horror-scopes.

When the werewolf hunter put his fingers into the werewolf's mouth to see how many teeth it had got, what did the werewolf do?
The werewolf closed its mouth to see how many fingers the hunter had.

What is written on the gravestone of Frankenstein's monster?
Rust in peace.

What is a monster's favourite breakfast cereal?
Dreaded wheat.

What did Dracula ask the undertaker?
'Do you deliver?'

What steps should you take if you meet a vampire?
Very long ones.

What should you sing at the Abominable Snowman's birthday party?
'Freeze a jolly good fellow. . .'

What is a vampire's favourite breakfast cereal?
Ready Neck.

What does a monster call his parents?
Deady and mummy.

If you want to join the Dracula fan club all you have to do is send him your name and address – and a blood sample.

Why do skeletons drink a lot of milk?
Because it's good for the bones.

Why do monsters tend to forget everything you say to them?
Because it goes in one ear and out the others.

BOY: Mum, what's a werewolf?
MOTHER: *Be quiet and comb your face.*

Why did Dracula never marry?
Because he loved in vein.

What does a ghost enjoy?
Being shrouded in mystery.

How did King Kong escape from his cage?
He used a monkey wrench.

Why did the skeleton stop going to parties?
He got tired of people hanging their hats and coats on him.

What do Hungarian ghosts eat?
Ghoulash.

The monster boss said to his monster secretary: 'I want you to type these twenty-four letters, go and get me a cup of coffee, nip down to the bank for some money, tell the managing monster that I would like a meeting with him, organize my trip to America, tell . . .'

'Just a minute!' said the secretary monster, 'I've only got three pairs of hands!'

Why didn't the skeleton go to the dance?
Because he had no body to go with.

What do you call a twenty stone monster who's been carrying a thirty stone monster all day?
Tired.

What kind of mistake does a ghost make?
A boo-boo.

Why should vampires never be trusted?
Because they are fly-by-nights.

Which monster has the best hearing?
The eeriest.

What do abominable snowparents have?
Chill-dren.

LITTLE MONSTER: Mum, I've brought a friend home for dinner.
MOTHER MONSTER: *That's nice, dear. Put him in the freezer, we'll have him next week.*

DOCTOR TO WITCH: I think you're looking better today. Tomorrow you can get out of bed for a spell.

How do you stop a werewolf from attacking you?
Throw a stick and say 'Fetch, boy!'

Who did the boy ghost take to the pictures?
His ghoulfriend.

Why did the monster go into the restaurant?
Because they were charging only £5 per head — he ordered four.

Why shouldn't you grab a werewolf by its tail?
It may be the werewolf's tail, but it could be your end.

What animal does a vampire like best?
A giraffe (just think of all that neck!)

Why did the skeleton break off his engagement?
Because his heart was not in it.

What do you get if you cross a vampire with a car?
A monster that attacks vehicles and sucks out all their petrol.

Why did the ghost love his girlfriend?
Because she was boo-tiful.

What is a vampire's favourite dance?
The fangdango.

What do you call a werewolf in sheep's clothing?
A were-wool-f.

Why did Frankenstein's monster give up boxing?
He didn't want to spoil his looks.

FIRST MONSTER: Today I am going to eat the city of Peking. Would you like to join me for dinner?
SECOND MONSTER: *No, thanks. I don't like Chinese food.*

What did Dr Jekyll say to Mr Hyde?
'Don't look now, I'm changing.'

Why did the monster at the circus ask for more money?
Because he had a lot of mouths to feed.

What did the monsters do at the wedding?
They toasted the bride and groom.

What did the werewolf eat after the dentist had seen to his teeth?
The dentist.

How does a ghost look when it is worried?
Grave.

Why was Dracula lost on the motorway?
He was looking for the main artery.

What do you call a monster that is twenty feet
high, with large teeth and horrible claws?
Sir.

FIRST MONSTER: Yesterday a tramp came to my
  door begging for food. He said he hadn't had
  a bite for four days.
SECOND MONSTER: *What did you do?*
FIRST MONSTER: I bit him.

What frozen food company is run by monsters?
Fiendus Foods.

How does a werewolf greet his victim?
He says: 'How do you do, I'm pleased to eat you.'

How would you describe a punk ghost?
A real cool ghoul.

Which ghost made friends with the three bears?
Ghouldilocks.

NURSE: Excuse me, doctor, the Invisible Man is waiting for you.
DOCTOR: *Tell him I can't see him.*

FIRST MONSTER: Who was that lady I saw you with last night?
SECOND MONSTER: *That was no lady, that was my dinner.*

Why was the dead person taken to the hospital in a car?
Because he was a car-case.

What's a vampire's favourite dance?
The vaults.

What sort of society would a vampire join?
A blood group.

How do ghosts repair their clothes?
They use invisible mending.

What would you call a baby witch?
A Halloweenie.

How do undertakers tie up their shoelaces?
They use a wreath knot.

A professor of music was researching the life and works of Mozart. One day he visited the grave of the famous musician − only to hear the sound of tearing paper coming from within. He found a crowbar and managed to open the grave. Inside was Mozart tearing up music manuscripts.

'Are you Mozart?' asked the professor.

'Yes, I am,' came the reply.

'But I thought you were dead − what are you doing tearing up all the music?'

Mozart looked up and said: 'I'm de-composing.'

What do you call a witch from another planet? *A flying sorcerer.*

What's a vampire's favourite game?
Bat-minton.

How did the man monster propose to the lady monster?
He said: 'I'd like your hand, hand, hand, hand in marriage.'

What do mummies use to paint their fingers?
Nile varnish.

What does a ghost order at a snack bar?
A sa-limy sandwich.

What did the mummy say to his girlfriend?
'Em-balmy about you.'

How do you make a skeleton laugh?
Tickle his funny bone.

What did the werewolf say to his victim?
'It's been nice gnawing you.'

What do you call a big hairy gorilla wearing a dress?
Queen Kong.

What do you call a bull with green eyes, fluorescent horns and breathing fire through its nostrils?
Horror-bull.

Why did the undertaker chop up the corpses?
He wanted them to rest in pieces.

What's a skeleton's favourite musical instrument?
A trombone.

What do you get if you cross a ghost with a spider?
A creepy crawlie.

What keeps Dracula's house guests awake?
His coffin.

What's a monster's favourite party game?
Swallow my leader.

Why is a vampire hunter like a knocked-out boxer?
Because he is out for the Count.

Why did King Kong join the army?
To learn about gorilla warfare.

What is a monster ape's favourite aeroplane?
King Kong-corde.

What do you say to a giant ape who has just won a prize?
'Kongratulations.'

What do werewolves write on their Christmas cards?
'Best vicious of the season.'

NICOLA: What is five inches long, red and black, with hairy claws?
MICHAEL: *I don't know. What is five inches long, red and black, with hairy claws?*
NICOLA: I don't know, either — but there's one crawling up your back!

Why did the monster stop the ghost from marrying his daughter?
Because he had no visible means of support.

What would you call a ghost who lived in the desert?
The shriek of Araby.

A fiend in need is a fiend indeed.

How do you know that Dracula has been in your fruit bowl?
There are fang marks in the blood oranges.

What is a ghost's favourite type of show?
A phantomime.

What name did the witch give to her cooking pot?
It was called-Ron.

Why did the male monster like the female monster?
It was love at first bite.

Why did the female monster like the male monster?
It was love at first fright.

Who referees the monsters' game of cricket?
The vumpire.

What did the monsters call their baby girl?
Norah Bone.

Where did the Abominable Snowman meet his wife?
At the snow ball.

What do you call a ghost doctor?
A surgical spirit.

What happens when a witch loses her temper?
She flies off the handle.

Where do undertakers go for their holidays?
Gravesend.

What does a monster like for breakfast?
Legs and bacon.

Where do undertakers go for their holidays?
Bury.

What is the Australian for 'undertaker'?
Digger.

How do skeletons communicate with each other?
They use the tele-bone.

What do you call a monster ape in China?
Hong Kong.

How do you make a witch scratch?
Take away her W.

A circus came to town and displayed a most
unusual two-headed monster — it only had
one head.

Why did the witch fail her examinations?
She couldn't spell properly.

What is pink, has a curly tail and drinks blood?
A hampire.

What is fearsome, hairy and drinks from the wrong side of a glass?
A werewolf with hiccups.

What does Count Dracula call his coffin?
His snuff box.

What is a monster's favourite ballet?
Swamp Lake.

What do sea monsters eat?
Fish and ships.

What do land monsters eat?
Fish and chaps.

What do you call a nervous witch?
A twitch.

How would you flatten a ghost?
Hit him with a spirit level.

How do you know when a skeleton is upset?
He gets rattled.

How does Dracula like to eat meat?
In grave-y.

What did the flea say when it walked down a
werewolf's back and eventually reached the
tail?

'THIS IS THE END.'

JOKE BOOKS

If you enjoyed reading all the hilarious jokes in this book,
perhaps you ought to try some more of our zany joke books.
They are available in bookshops or they can be ordered directly
from us. Just complete the form below and enclose the right
amount of money and the books will be sent to you at home.

☐ THE WOOLLY JUMPER JOKE BOOK	Peter Eldin	£1.25
☐ MORE BROWNIE JOKES		£1.25
☐ THE WOBBLY JELLY JOKE BOOK	Jim Eldridge	£1.25
☐ A VERY MICE JOKE BOOK	John Hegarty	£1.25
☐ THE JOKE-A-DAY FUN BOOK	Janet Rogers	£1.50
☐ THE CRAZY JOKE BOOK STRIKES BACK	Janet Rogers	£1.50
☐ THE ELEPHANT JOKE BOOK	Katie Wales	£1.00
☐ FLOELLA'S FUNNIEST JOKES	Floella Benjamin	£1.25

If you would like to order books, please send this form, and the
money due to:
ARROW BOOKS, BOOKSERVICE BY POST, PO BOX 29,
DOUGLAS, ISLE OF MAN, BRITISH ISLES. Please enclose
a cheque or postal order made out to Arrow Books Ltd for the
amount due including 30p per book for postage and packing
both for orders within the UK and for overseas orders.

NAME ....

ADDRESS ....

....

Please print clearly.